Love, Loss and the Hope In Between

Paul Garland

BookLeaf Publishing

India | USA | UK

Presentation by *BookLeaf Publishing*

Web: www.bookleafpub.com

E-mail: info@bookleafpub.com

ISBN: 9789363314214

First edition 2024

To Emily, who loves me now and forever

*And to Nana, who loved me until Emily
came along.*

ACKNOWLEDGEMENT

There are so many people who are deserving of thanks for being part of the journey to get here.

Many thanks to those who encouraged me along the way, or inspired poems, or were just "there".

Thank you to Jen for being my test reader, to Dr. Plummer for encouraging me when I needed it, the members of the Michigan Writer's Group for their critiques, and you for being willing to step into my world.

To all the librarians over the years who encouraged me to read, to teachers who told me to save my poetry, to the select few who have read over the years, thank you.

And lastly, to Robert Frost for making New England such a beautiful place to grow in, my eternal thanks.

First Day Of School

Not everyone can say that their first day
Was immortalized in print
But for better or worse
The entire town and maybe those around
Were treated to a big, beautiful picture of me
On the front page of the paper.

My teacher and I were captured in color
My tears big and salty and plentiful
My teacher looking like she was regretting
Her decision to become a kindergarten teacher
Instead of going into banking
Like her parents had suggested.

By the time my mother came and got me
The tears had finally dried
And I bounded out of school happy
Delighted that my day had gone so well
And already looking forward to the next day
And seeing my teacher again.

My mother asked me quietly with a smile
How my day had gone, had I had fun?
I told her that yes, I had loved it all
Played games, had snacks, took a rest
Told how my teacher read books

And let us draw with crayons.

So no problems? She probed me again
None. I told her, staring out the window
She chuckled and handed me the paper
Isn't that you? You look upset.
I took in the picture, staring at my face
"Haven't you heard, I was so happy I cried?"

She didn't believe me. Which isn't surprising.
What IS a surprise to me
Is the fact that 25 years later, I wondered
What happened to that teacher?
And using the magic of the internet, and
Facebook
I found her name, and reached out.

Of course, I remember you! She replied
You were in my very first class! Hello after all
these years!
And we reminisced about the photo
And the changes over the decades
She told me about almost being a banker.

I wonder sometimes, what I would have done
Had my mother just handed me the paper
With my crying face above the fold
And patted my head and asked, Rough day?
Would I have had such a great story to tell
Of my almost banker teacher and me?

Summer Magic

We ran with a rhythm all our own,
Sneakers pounding time against the grass
Drumming the beat to our new-sung song
The summer we met after camp

Slipping, tripping, stepping, stopping
Each path we took a journey
A search for the elusive answer-
What now? What's next?

Our youthful hearts on the move
Making our way to teenager-hood
Taking each step so carelessly
As we left childish games behind

Anxious for the new, now, next
Wanting everything we did not have
Desiring things we didn't understand

Content in the knowledge that we two
Alone in a world full of adults
Shared a secret nobody else knew-
Summer was truly magic

And the last three weeks before school
Held the greatest spells,
The deepest charms
The rarest of incantations
Voiced new each morning from our throats
And launched headlong into the sun-
The mantra we shared
With only each other:
What shall we do today?

Biking to the Moon

Is there anything better when you are a kid
Than the moment your parent lets go of the bike
And you fly away, wobbly, but in control
Pointing your wheels any way that you like?

The street hums beneath you, a blur and a path
Leading you forward wherever it goes
Adventure is waiting, and calling your name
You pedal, and seize it, and follow your nose

Past houses you've known your entire life
In your mind now spectators
Of this special event
Transformed to elaborate parts of the story
You'll tell your mom
When she asks where you went

I went to the moon! You'll proudly proclaim
Saw meteors, rockets and aliens too
They chased me but I was just too fast for them
Then I turned at the corner
And came back to you

She'll smile and nod, ask if you want a snack
And dismiss your escape as a fine afternoon

But deep in your heart you will already know
What is waiting for you
And your bike
On the moon!

Fitting In

I remember that day as clear as if it were now
You, sending me to camp
Telling me to be good
Play nice
Make friends
Fit in.
Like fitting in was the goal, the entire purpose of
the summer
Forget learning to ride a horse
Make a craft
Pay attention to the beauty that is around you
Just
FIT IN
I came back from camp a failure,
unsure why "fitting in" was so important
Especially given the very tiny chance
of ever seeing those campers again
Would, in fact, be unlikely to even be
remembered
Yeah, that one kid- he just seemed to "fit in"
And it made me
Sad
Not for me! For YOU!
Suddenly I understood why your shoulders
perpetually

drooped at the end of the day
Why you dreaded to go to work
Why your hair was turning gray at only 35
You were still trying to "fit in"
Trying to find your "you" shaped space
in a world so fractured and broken
That you'd need to break off pieces of yourself
Just to come close to "fitting"
And I knew, in that moment
That I would never "fit in"
I would never accept a world that broke me,
that was not content to accept, no room for me
As me
Because why should I be the one
To give up my self
To break off pieces
Losing them, losing
Me
To try and find a spot in a world that didn't want
me?
How much better to choose instead
A me that the world wanted
A me the world would make room for
A me the world would watch and know
Deep down
That it would never fit in with me.

Finding My Voice

Sing! Said the teacher, waving her hand
Sing like the birds in the tree!
And we opened our mouths and everyone sang
Everyone that is, but me.

I tried to sing, but nothing came from my mouth
Just the tiniest sad puff of air
Sing! Said the teacher, from deep down inside!
But I looked, and I found nothing there.

You must sing! Cried the teacher,
Or you cannot stay!
And sadly I walked out of the room
I wanted so badly to join in with the songs
But my lack of voice filled me with gloom

I went to the brook and I asked the brook why?
Why can you sing when I don't?
Because, said the brook, I sing with glee
Until you are happy, you won't.

I asked the tree branches
What gave them the song
That they whispered all day and all night.
We go with the flow of the wind, they replied
Let go, just relax, stop your fight!

The birds sang above me, so I asked them next-
What gives you your beautiful voice?
We're flyers, they said, we float and we flap
It's the way we were made- we've no choice!

That night, I asked all the stars up above
What's the secret to your stellar flight?
They twinkled and sparkled and finally replied:
We don't know- but to us it feels right.

So I sat and I thought, and I tried hard to feel
To relax, and be happy inside of my head
And I opened my mouth,
And I took a deep breath,
Then I went and played trumpet instead!

Ten For A Day

For one day, just one day, I'd like to return
Back to the age of oh, ten or so
That was a time of such simple happiness
A bike, a friend and off I'd go

We'd explore the world around us, amazed
At all the new things we'd see
When malls were bustling, and candy was cheap
And we felt so wild and free

We hid under our desks in school, like a game
When the sirens would all go off
And nobody moved or made any sounds
We'd muffle our laughter or coughs

And the funny thing is, we felt safer that way
Even knowing that if the bombs came
If we were out in a field or under our desks
We'd all die off just the same

But at ten you don't register things like that
You just think it's cozy and cool
Sitting in the class, reading your own book
Instead of learning the same stuff at school

And you look 'cross the room, and smile at your
friends
And blush when that one girl smiles too

Perhaps there's a reason you'd want to survive
If someone that cute could like you?

After school you go riding with all of your friends
Another bomb drill in the past
Til shadows grow long, as the sun slowly sets
And you make your way home at last

Tomorrow you'll get up and do things again
The same way you did them today
And the time will go by, and you'll one day be old
And you'll long to be ten- for one day.

The Journey

We moved a lot when I was a kid
Seems like every summer was a new house
A new chance to make new friends
A new way to look at the world
Everything "new"
As if throwing that word in front
Of everything would make it all right again.

To a ten year old, new is exciting
New is an adventure, an invitation to explore
More than it is a reminder of what you left
Who you left
Why you left.

By the time you are 13 and on your sixth school
New is no longer fun
New is in fact a perpetual anchor
A label you wear everywhere you go
Alerting people of your difference
A different way of talking
A different way of dressing
Different tastes in food
In music
In friends

By the time you are 16, and unpacking
Again
In your eleventh different house
You find that you hate the word new
You only want the old
The familiar
The known

And life won't play nice, and let you stay
Instead, you move again
And Again
And suddenly, college is behind you
And it's time for another move
And you decide

This is it.

And you put your feet down
To stop your momentum
And you decided where you are now
Will be home for the rest of your life
Until one day
It isn't

Because you've met somebody
Different than anyone else you ever knew
Who makes you want to travel
Beside them and see the world
Through their eyes

So you take a step

And then a leap

And the journey begins.

Summer Camp By Choice

The drive to camp was quiet
You didn't want to talk
You thought I was making a mistake, again
By picking this job for the summer.

You remembered my first time at camp
The tearful phone calls home
The letters that I wrote
Describing my solitude and pain

And you couldn't decide if this time
I'd call you to come get me
Or just set out walking for home
Within the first two days

Your silence chilled the car
Until you exploded into words
Heated, pointed, driving
Asking me again for the thousandth time
If I was ABSOLUTELY SURE?

I tried not to show it outwardly
But inside I was laughing
Excited to begin the summer
For the first time in a long time

Excited to be somewhere new

I tried to explain it to you
In a way you could understand
That my job would be to help
Children who like myself
Were coming to camp to "fit in"

Showing them that they, themselves,
Were the shapers of the world
The makers of tomorrow
The advocates of what it means
To "fit in"

And my hope was simple-
That they would come to camp
Find themselves, and some friends
And having made that discovery
They would change the world.

Sounds of Growth

In the still of the night, I lie
And listen to the sounds of growth
Since I cannot hear the ones inside
I turn my ears to the noises
Made by the plants outside
And I wonder how it must be
To bend to the stresses around you
Just letting them slip by
Moving you but not breaking
Shifting you slightly like a branch
But springing back to be
Just the way you were
Before being touched by stresses.

I am trying.
I am learning.
I am reaching.
I am growing.
Silently.

I have discovered I grow best
When I keep the noises
Inside
Unlike the world outside
Where every breeze brings protest
From the branches it moves
Every gust causes whispers of resignation
From blades of grass used to being
Separate and tall.
Even animals give voice
To their inner thoughts and changes
As they grow-
Tiny chirps become raucous cries
When birds learn to use their wings
Why should I be any different?

So forgive my groans
My tears
My dark days of sullen-faced resignation

Embrace my joyful shouts
Collect my laughs
Savor those moments of murmured pleasure

They are my sounds of growth.

Abandoned

I came home from my time abroad at last
And you didn't come to meet me
The whole of the family was all there at the gate
Except the face I wanted to see

Can't say I was surprised that you stayed home
Since you no longer spoke to our folks
But you'd promised you'd stay til I returned
And told you my stories and jokes

But we walked in the door, the house eerily dark
Your room completely cleaned out
And the letter you left saying you were gone
Quickly removed any last doubt

You abandoned me there with all the mess
And the fallout of choices you made
You couldn't be bothered to wait one more hour
Your leaving could not be delayed

I'll never understand what broke the last straw
And caused you to steal away
But I know that our parents were caught by surprise
When you left our home that day
I tried to still reach you, to stay in the loop
Visiting you at your work
And hearing your tales of what you had done
While seeing you as a bit of a jerk

Later, again, you would destroy my trust
You'd spurn, curse and try to hurt me
But the truth is you chose to cut yourself off
From the one who loved you for free

And now as we both make our way in the world
I wonder at times where you are
I still, foolishly wish all the good things to you
Even though you are gone now, so far

Abandonment starts without saying goodbye
And leaving a hole when you go
But I keep that hole open, the door is quite wide
And I'd welcome you back, so you know.

Finding My People

The old door creaked loudly, protesting as it opened,
Revealing an aged yellow carpet leading out of sight
On impossibly tall steps with a carved wood rail
The air was still and filled with dust and heat
I wondered again what was I doing there
I had no business barging into this place
Making myself known among these people
Thinking myself ready to be one of them
And yet
And yet, I was ready.
I was tired of being alone with my thoughts
Sick of making myself crazy
Looking for where I fit in
Dying inside from a lack of creative outlet
And besides, if I messed up badly enough
I just wouldn't come back and never see them again!

I reached the top of the stairs
And pushed open the door
A roiling cascade of noise assaulted me
Voices of various volume and pitch
Rising and falling and dipping and soaring
Spilling over each other in a cavalcade of creativity
As they mangled lines, or hummed a tune
Tried vainly to look exactly like what the director
That unseen arbiter of allotment who would decide
Which of us were worthy of working with
And which would be consigned to lurk

In the darkness behind the curtain
Or sit spellbound in the seats
Counting the mistakes and thinking
I could have done better
If given the chance.

One by one we performed, we quoted, we sung
The lyrics we were given, the lines we were handed
The roles we were inspected for, as if the fit
Of our soul to the shape of the character was visible
And weighed by the director
Even as it remained invisible to us
One by one we were thanked for our time
In a manner both final and fair
Until at last the entirety of the room had a chance
To be heard, and seen, and weighed
And the director called out a list of people
Who left the room
To the rest of us, he smiled and said
Hello. You've made it in. Welcome to the family.
I sat silent, sure of a mistake
Afraid if I moved he would remember
That he had meant
To include me in the goodbye.
Instead, he stopped and handed me a script
And patted me on my shoulder and said
I know it doesn't seem like much
But it's a heck of a fun part to get your feet wet on
And he stopped,
Took in my confusion
And said
Doesn't it feel good to have found your people?

My Favorite Part of Falling In Love

My favorite part of falling in love
Is the very first moment
When it dawns on you what is happening,
That you have let your guard down enough to notice
Someone outside yourself
The first frisson of attraction that,
Like a startled cat
Or a hidden electric fence rudely discovered
Tingles so sublimely up your spine
That tingle before the ultimate tangle
That heartbeat before the untimely heartbreak
That moment you lose yourself
And just don't care
That moment when for just the slightest of seconds
The world is ok, and everything is fine
Even you
You see yourself as the other person sees you
Looking past their faults
As they extend the same grace to you
And knowing that even though they don't see
Your flaws
Your cracks
Your failures
They wouldn't care if they should see them
That is the moment I treasure
The moment I hang on to like

A talisman against the dark
Knowing forever after that even if the love is doomed
Even if the relationship turns toxic and cold
For one brief golden moment
I was enough

First Fight

I remember our first fight
Words hurled like overripe fruits
Aimed not so much to harm as to mark
To express the emotions
Coursing through our veins
That we were too immature to express calmly,
rationally

I can see it all, still-
The hatred in our faces, twisted and raw
The pointed fingers
The flashing eyes, flying hair
I can even hear it in my heart, the wind of time
through the holes from the barbs
Unhealed after all this time.

I wince as I recall particular words and accusations
Connecting with your soft spirit
Piercing your gentle heart
Tearing chunks of your self away
Knowing, even then that what I was doing was killing
The very thing I loved most in the world
And not caring about anything except
the fact that you were doing it too.

I remember, I grieve, I bring
Scene after scene to mind-
A cacophony of self-flagellation

As if the renewed pain could erase
the fight from history

Could rebirth the love we once shared
Knowing all the while
That it will never be
That it was never meant to be
And I remember it all-

Except what we fought about.

Impossible To Win At War

"It's impossible," she asserted,
eyes flashing, hair shining
"You cannot tell someone
what you truly think of them
And remain polite."
She paused,
as if sifting her thoughts for the certainty
That her declaration was true in all cases,
or just this.

I waited patiently
Only needing a last cigarette and a blindfold
to complete the mental image
of facing judge, jury, executioner

And being found wanting
Lacking in her eyes
The end was mercifully quick, yet still
poignantly painful.

"You've changed," she proclaimed laughing
Nervous yet sure of herself
"You used to take exception so easily to
everything
At what I said, how I said it

Even
The way I looked as I said it."

I spoke, reluctantly, uneager to be drawn
Into her game;
"And now?"

She smiled, suddenly compassionate for perhaps
the first time,
Her hand rested on my arm
Fingers cold as her words
"You?
Now?
Now you are no longer a challenge,
No longer a cypher to be broken.
You are what I've made you be
And THAT
just isn't enough for me anymore."

She rose to leave, her handiwork done and
abandoned like some child's once-favorite toy
Now simply a plaything
with no meaning any longer.

I gave her the exit, left the last line of our life
together on her lips
No longer willing to fight for a losing side in a
war I never remember signing up for.

There are certain conflicts that exist just because
someone willed it so
And since the stronger will was hers
It had been her battlefield
That I was conscripted to,
to lose.

Colorless

When life has lost its color
And again you are, inevitably, alone
Remind yourself that once you held
The entirety of my existence in your arms
And for a moment, a breath of time
We orbited each other like birds
Fluttering, singing, circling
But never touching
Doomed by life or fate or luck
To meet, and admire from afar
The very one that we found
Not flaws, per se
But a sense of "wrongness"
When close
What was it, I wonder
That we both saw in the other
The thing that spoke to us with hope
That evaporated when examined
In the bright light of day?
I will go on wondering
As I never have felt
The same as I did with you
With any other

Carefree
Colorful
Clueless
Clueless about the fact that I
Was not enough for you, not bright enough to be
with you
Not small enough to fit your world view
But you had your faults too
If only I could remember them
For some measure of comfort, and calm
And color

The Open Cabinet

My house has a party trick
A silly thing really
But it makes me smile each time
A sign from the house to me
That things are as they should be.

Every time I shut a door
Another opens.
Not being metaphorical, here
The reality is that something in my house
Seems determined to maintain
An open atmosphere

As if the sole use of the door that pops open
Is to be responsible for
Greeting every spirit, or soul, or ghost
That crosses the threshold
And settles in to visit.

I could fix the cabinet easily enough-
Fairly quickly too-
But the fact of the matter remains
That I like the idea
Of being so welcoming

I hardly think about the fact that the door
Opens anymore
I just note it in the corner
Of my mind's eye
And continue with my day.

The most wonderful thing about it
Is the pernicious thing
Won't perform its parlor trick
For just any old person-
In fact, just for me

As if my house and I have agreed
That we both
Are open to visitors as long
As they can understand
Some doors will remain closed

Permanently.

The Remembered You

I wish I could be angry with you, if I'm honest
Could coldly cut you out of my heart
The way you cut me out of your life
Wielding the sharp knife of your tongue
Flaying my affections with abandon
But I cannot.
I cannot forgive myself for the failure to separate
The lack of acceptance of closure
You threw carelessly over
Us
Your contempt for all we shared a blanket
admission
That we were never me and you
But me and my vision of what you could be-
A hoped-for rendition of faithfulness
Connecting with me in a way that I needed
Linked so thoroughly in my deluded mind

That I could only see you
As perfect.

I wish I could get back to that place
The time when I saw you as everything right in
the world
The center of my happiness
My reason to get up in the morning
But I know that if I found my way back there
Knowing what I know now
I'd see the cracks in your facade
That I made myself blind to the first time around
Shadows
Hiding your flaws
Helping you pass for a complete person
Blinding me to what I know now is truth
That I then saw as quirky
Granting you grace that you did nothing to earn
Nothing to expect
Nothing to even deserve
But I gave it anyway
Like a fool
In love
With the idea, if not the reality.
I wish I could go back
But the remembered you would not be there
Anymore than you are here
And I would lose you
All over again.

First to Last

In the middle of the night I awaken
Startled at the amount of "firsts"
We have shared in just three years:
First kiss
First dance
First fight
First heartbreak

And I find myself wondering why
We mark the beginnings of things
So religiously
While totally ignoring the "lasts"
That litter our lives like fallen stars

The last kiss
The last goodbye
The last time I got to call you mine

I wonder at the audacity of spirit it takes
To constantly, consciously restart-
To celebrate the beginning while ignoring
The end

What makes the start of anything better than the
end?

What makes the renewal of optimism
Any more noble, or noteworthy
Than the solid realization
That what we hoped would happen didn't
Again?

I'd much rather dwell on the firsts
The rapidity of my heartbeat
As our lips drifted towards each other
Mind whirling with the possibility
That THIS time I'll actually kiss you
Rather than chicken out-

The first time I held you feeling that you
Were suddenly not just someone
Who needed a hug
But someone I wanted to keep close to me
To hold on to the beauty I found
In you.

But life doesn't allow us the kindness
To focus on the firsts without also remembering
the lasts
Like some great scale in the cosmos
Will cease to exist unless we balance
Our life full of highs and lows
By carefully examining
Both sides of life.

And even as I think of these things
I find myself left with the overwhelming desire
To see you, to tell you one more time
Thank you for being all of my "firsts"
Even as you are my first "last".

Class

We found each other without a crowd, I liked to say
She didn't find it humorous in the least
The idea that there were only
Three people signed up for the class,
And the teacher canceled
And forgot to tell anyone
And we were the only ones who showed up
Making awkward small talk
In a huge empty lecture hall
As if it were the world's oddest coffee shop
Minus the Lattes.
Fast forward two months and we were getting lattes
A regular event after each class or lecture
Our way of keeping the magic
Of that first meeting alive
In a desperate attempt to avoid
What we both already knew was coming,
As if empty laughs and full cups
Could chase away the fact
That we had nothing in common
And too many differences to compile.
The idea does bring me pause
As I try to imagine how long a list
Those differences would be,
And what would wind up being at the top
Of the list.
Would the biggest difference between us be
Personality?

Taste in friends?
Favorite foods, or something even more
Banal?
No matter, now. The inevitable split
Occurred long ago
And we have charted separate paths in life
Moved on in our varied circles
Left those cold, awkward coffee dates behind
And yet,
At times,
I find myself wondering
Whatever happened to the third person
Who registered for the class?

Unwanted

"You don't have what I want"
As if love were simply a store display
Enticingly arrayed to draw you in
Seduce you
Capture the senses
Make you FEEL… more
Rather than make you BE…whole.

She'd never told me what she wanted
Relying instead on me to guess
Waiting for me to just know what she lacked
Waiting for me to grasp the spark;
The eternal quest for her satisfaction
Deferred to my care
Carelessly draped upon me
Impossibly weighty for all its vagueness.

Perhaps if she had simply stated it
Said "I want…" at least once instead of standing
Staring disappointedly at me as I failed
Again
To be the piece in her puzzle, the link in her chain
The answer to the hole in her world.

Somewhere between "hello" and
"You don't have what I want"
There was a moment I must have missed
A signal that all was not right
That burned, bright and clear in the haze of night.
I wondered if I might
Just maybe
Have been what she wanted if I had noticed earlier
If I had seen her unhappiness
Her lack.

But I have come to realize, as I look at the wreck
The tangle of emotions and loss
That it was not me who was not enough
It was not my love she wanted
My heart she craved, my emotions she valued
And as such, I could never have what she wanted:

What she wanted, in a nutshell-
To be daddy's girl again
Just for one afternoon to be the princess again
The shining star that only glowed
Brighter for the attention,
Her fire consuming everything around her
That would be what she wanted.

To be the prize one guarded instead
Of being the one guarding the prize
Her overwhelming need to center everything
Around and about her in a blindly, blindingly
Child-like obliviousness.

Not that she cared that much what others thought of
her
Rather that she cared what SHE thought of herself
What SHE measured herself as, falling short
Standing on tiptoes in a vain attempt at worth.
"You just didn't do it for me"
Dismissive, cold to the last
As if I were some magic elixir disappointing
Discouraging, despairing of desire, delineating the
Dash between If and Then
A broken computer program.

It wasn't that she was emotionless
Or devoid of feelings
It was me
I was at fault, I was to blame, I was the problem
Never her, never the grown-up princess
Of Daddy's dreams.

I was the one she felt had failed,
and was to be blamed
And was to be discarded for not
Meeting her impossible
Unspoken

Unspecified standards.

I was the glitch, the itch, the patch of poison ivy
That she had stepped in
And couldn't get away from fast enough
And I wanted so much to just ask her
Just....once
What about me? What about what I wanted?
But it wouldn't have mattered.

She'd already dismissed me, and was gone.

Disappointed

I wish there were words in my heart
Able to express the sentiment of disappointment
Your lack of action has caused me.

You choose the easy path, you always have
And if that means I am left behind on your
journey
That's just the way it has to be.

But it hurts nonetheless, your disregard
Your callous mental discarding of our
connection
Spurred by your need to be yourself.

To "find" yourself, whatever you mean by that
Its vagueness both unnerving and menacing at
once
As if the search was the final goal

I wonder—
You have made it to your age
Without taking stock of all the things
That make you- you
And I suppose you don't like yourself much
Because, truth to tell, there is much to like

Not just about yourself, but about the us that was
The us that once was a we, was you and I

And I imagine scenarios that never were
In a bid to create that which will now never be
Trading the pain of yesterday for tomorrow

Putting off admitting the crushing defeat
For the fading hopeful wish
That tomorrow will bring
A new choice of words to give you

So that you will know, with no doubts possible
Exactly what I think
Of what you have done to our past
And why forgiveness will never be in the cards.

Orbital Mechanics

I had forgotten how it felt to love
That comfort, that fuzzy feeling
The way your brain refuses to go one day
Without thinking about that person
Without missing them next to you
And then, I met you
Well, noticed you first- both of us
Too shy, shell-shocked or battle weary
To make the first move, relying instead
On an unreliable mediary
To relay our mutual interest.
Which, when that failed, we seized
Our chances as we could
Bravely throwing ourselves into alignment
Hoping the pull of gravity
Would keep us in each other's orbit.
Shocked when it worked,
Surprised when each found the other
As fragile as ourselves,
As frightened as the other
But equally willing to try again.
And now, we travel as one
A pair of twin stars orbiting along
Feeding each other's brightness
Reflecting each other's light
Making the sum of our parts better
For being the whole.

Curtain

How can the world be anything but a stage
When we are our own worst critics?
When the everyday follies and foibles
Of our simply attempting to survive
Translate so well to tired vaudeville routines
And corny, dated, one-liners

Delivered by the hardened comics
That exist behind our eyes and peer
Squinting through the smoky haze
Of our stress-addled brains at the reflection
Cast upon the surface of life's mirror-
A funhouse version of self

We flit across the stage, bereft
Of any sense of self-preservation
Not the kind that makes sure we survive
But the kind that says WE- our personal self
Our way we see ourselves in the quiet inside
Our vision of self is preserved

Quickly we change our faces, painting
A smile across our honest frown
Distancing ourselves from sadness
Only admitting to being less than our best

After someone else has been brave enough
To admit their own failings

And yet, the admission does not embolden
It merely gives us permission to admit
To feelings, to lack of perfection, to that
That small crack in our perfect armor
The hole in our composure where the truth
Leaks out if we aren't careful

What would be so bad if we were to speak
If we were to admit just once, even once
That we are hurt, we're alone, we're scared
That we have measured ourselves and found
lack
Lack of strength, lack of ambition, lack of love
Do we think we lose something by sharing?

So bring down the curtain, end the play
I'm tired of pretending to be what I'm not
Too weary to dress myself up in the robe
Of the confident, capable, cultivated king
For today alone, I will be genuine
A tired man, a fool, perhaps. But..me.

Now I Notice

It's amazing what I notice now
That I have stopped looking only backwards
Since you lifted me from my darkness
And helped me stand next to you
Your hand holding mine
Directing me to see what you see
Especially in the mirror.

I see things I would have passed by before, things
That would have escaped my notice
Lost in my doldrums and blind
To the beauty of the world around me
Deaf to the music of the breeze
Numb to the feeling of being content
And simply feeling happy.

I will never know what you saw in me then
What you continue to see in me now
But I want you to know how very much
How intensely I thank you
For finding me in myself
For drawing me out again
And for glueing my parts back together

I still don't recognize myself totally
Like I'm almost my own forgotten relative
A face remembered from long ago
A voice I cannot recall

I rise each day,
Looking at myself in the mirror
Saying 'Oh THERE I am!'

And all the while, I hope
With every ounce of hope you've uncovered in me
That on some level I do the same
For you- show you your beauty
Your grace, your truth
Over and over, every day
For the rest of our lives.

Walking In Darkness

Walls around me, dark brick and stone
Soot-covered sentries of the old city
I wander through at night, alone
Noticing grime more than the pretty

It's solemn at night, a citadel
Of broken glass and rusted can
Perhaps it's somehow just as well
To be alone at night, a man

Exploring the backside of the known
Sharing the streets with ancient cats
Who argue that this place is their own
Regardless of if you give them pats

Frost said it best, I would have to think
Calling this an "acquaintance" with the night
This forging of a small sort of link
Between the soul and what lies beyond sight

Some think it sad, or lonely or wrong
To wander alone through the darkness
But I find the night has its own sort of song
That one hears only when one's restless

It calls the explorer, the searcher for that
Which exists merely just beyond reach
And the night and city, and angry old cat
All have many lessons to teach

I wander the darkness, mind open wide
To learn what the city can show
No friend or lover walking by my side
Only faded lamplight for the glow

Stark walls around me, my echoes rebound
Where soot-covered sentries still stand
I wander til morning light spills over the ground
And the city continues as planned.

The people who wander in daylight appear
Off to their jobs, their lives, their days
And I marvel as marvelous noise hits my ear
And the colors that dazzle my gaze.
And I wonder, again, why I love the dark
With its limited palette of grays
Are the differences really all that stark
That night feels safer than days?

Canal For Frogs

My host family showed me a canal
That was home to an incredible story
A long ago King had it built, it was said
To thank the frogs of his kingdom
For keeping the pests from the rice.

It is a beautiful place- low, cool, green
And the sounds of the city are kept at bay
By the seemingly endless bamboo
Rising on each side of the canal
A green curtain of nature

To be sure, there are dozens of frogs
Several toads and a duck or two
Enjoying the water, or the mossy rocks
Harmonizing with the trickling canal
Their voices croaking softly

I think to myself, it must have been nice
To have a King so kind and caring
Worried about even the smallest subjects
Regardless of their ability to pay
Taxes, or even indeed obeisance

I wonder for a moment if his people
Were as well taken care of as the frogs
If the king made sure they were housed
Ensured their safety and comfort
In return for their loyal support

I ask my host family if they know
And they smile politely behind their hands
Not quite laughing at the foolish kid
Who honestly, to this day prefers
The fable to the practical truth

After all, when you think about it,
Wouldn't it be a better world
When our leaders worried more
About being grateful to those
Who put them in leadership to begin with?

Lighthouse

It was dark before you found me-
Not the gray of twilight, dappled with stars,
But truly night; black, cold, isolated
But your smile, bright and warm and open-
All the things I wasn't at the time-
Your smile found me.
Your smile charmed me.
Your smile brought me back to the light
Forcing me, reluctant at first,
To release my hold on the weights of past failures
The memories that tied me down
The self-fulfilling prophecy of loneliness and despair.

But you held out your hand
And you smiled

Warming my soul
Creating a need
A hunger
To see that smile every day
For the rest of my life.
And deep inside my heart
In a room long neglected
Dusty from disuse
Crammed with crumpled wishes
That would never come to be spoken-
Deep in that chamber
A spark appeared.

Your acceptance and kindness
Working together with the last vestige of hope
Fanning the spark until it began to consume
The leftover scraps of yesterday
That littered the floor of my heart
Warming my soul
Sending heat to my brain
Changing me to become the person
I was always meant to be
The person I had hoped
To become
The person I needed to be

For you.

Growing Older Is A Cruel Mistress

Growing older is a cruel mistress
Draining happiness from all one does
As if jealous of the energy spent
On activities requiring more than oneself.

In youth, we hold the loneliness at bay
With imagined friends, or games, or dreams
That, as we age, suffer slow, inevitable deaths
Leaving cold emptiness in their wake.

Forgetful, we travel through life
Losing sight of the fact that we once held
The secret of happiness in loose fingers
Carelessly transporting treasure.

And when, inevitably, our grip loosens
Letting fall the sparkling crown of youth
We are often too busy just surviving
To mourn the departure of satisfaction;

To yearn for one last walk in wonder-
The friends of youth constant by our side,
We fail to notice the darkness invading
The meadows of our minds.

For if we were to notice the change-
If we for one moment could pause the headlong,
Heedless chase of the unattainable
We would shudder at what our lives become.

We would tremble at how much of ourselves
We were sacrificing in the futile quest
To grow up, to mature, to be more than we are
Just because others told us to.

And so we age, and we mature
Our bodies straining at what once we did
Effortlessly, easily, simply
That now is out of reach.

Why do we do it? Why do we leave it all
And chase the life that others prescribe
Why do we grow old, grow tired, grow past
What we once thought of as happiness?

Because, little one, we must
We must grow older, grow wiser, grow up
Or we would doom ourselves forever
To never change a thing.

Life is hard, and cold, and often lonely
Yes, it's true but not happily so
But life is also color and joy and oh so much
More than simply aging.

And that is the secret you see
That is the reason we must grow older
Because with age comes wisdom
And with wisdom, appreciation;

With appreciation comes the knowledge
That what life has taught
Was worthy of learning, whether we did or not
And that brings acceptance.

Perhaps

I woke to the world covered in crystals
The frost, thick as night, across the glass
The grass, long dead by now
Crowned with a glisten of white
Like a bride.

It made me smile to think of the world thus-
A cold, fragile lover
On her wedding day arrayed
With shining lights
Of glass.

And yet, the stillness, the lack of sound
No birdsong disrupted
No low noise of progress echoed
The air as still and quiet
As a tomb.

Was this the way death felt, I thought
When one is gone and in the grave
Removed from the world
The beat of their hearts
Forever stilled?

Do the dead look upon the world
Jealous of the movement
The noise of everyday life
Now for them nothing
But a memory?

Or perhaps to them the frost
Is nothing more than pretty
A reminder of the beauty
Life once held briefly
Before they departed?

Perhaps.

Loss

What is left after the loss heals?
Where exactly does the sorrow go?
What fills the cracks with meaning,
With sense, with worth?
How do we move on when our world
has stopped- and why
Doesn't my watch stop since you are no longer
there to orbit?
Your smile the sun
Your touch the cool moon
How can you ask me to soldier on, the
Sisyphean task of simply making it through
The day more than I can bear to even
contemplate?
For you, it must be easy- reduced to an
untouchable ideal
An idea of perfection still echoing in my empty
soul, winds of thought
Replacing the solid beat of my heart, so in tune
with yours
That it left when you did, leaving me hollow and
alone and empty
A drum without a beat, as useless as can be.
If you come back, we can pretend this was just a
vacation

A separation by events rather than by choice-
A break, a pause
And not the end, full stop, hard cut,
Screen full of THE END
We'll pretend it never happened, and move on
And continue
The way we were, hopeless, helpless Clueless
Happy in our delusions, blissful in our blindness
Afraid to admit that what we have
Is something we never had
And never can
Because to admit that would be to admit defeat,
To admit that the world should have colors that
Ours does not
Colors that would bring joy
To those around them
Just for being seen.
Since this was your doing, this sudden leaving,
This dissolution of US
You need to fix it.
Now.
Put us back together the way we used to be,
The way we are meant to be,
According to all our friends
Fitting together so tightly
There was no room for either of us
To be ourselves in the relationship
Unhealthy as that may have been
As sad as it made me

And even as lonely as it was
It felt right, at the time
And now
It doesn't.
I guess what it boils down to is that I now
understand
Why you left
And why you have to stay gone.

Enough

It's been a year
A year of mourning what was
Remembering
Rewriting conversations to make sense
Revisiting events to see if they could have gone
differently
Constantly searching for how it all went so wrong
So completely wrong.
And I have beat myself up
Broken and rebroken my own heart so many times
That all I have left to cry
Are words- all tears have dried and died long ago.
I still miss you
Somehow, I feel I always shall miss you
But I am stronger now
Able to stand on my own at last
Able to look at the past year and say
Enough
Enough pain
Enough loss
Enough misery
Just…enough.
And that is the thought I will hold
And carry with me into the new year
Just enough.
Each day will have just enough time to get what must
be done
Each smile will be just enough to cheer me

Each person I meet will be just enough to fill
A them-shaped hole in my world
And if I practice this enough,
If I learn to be content
If I make myself move on
By the end of next year
I hopefully will find that

I

Am just

Enough.

Distance Matters

It's not that I mind the quiet without you,
that lingering sense of self
That comes with being
The only heartbeat in the house.
I am growing comfortably familiar with
The creaks and groans of this old place
The noises made in an empty house giving life
To a lifeless room.

I sit in the dimming light each afternoon
and watch the sunset
Painting the house across the way with light
Even as my room descends into gray
Growing colder with each lost ray
Darkness kept at bay, my lamplight
Just enough to read by.

How nice it would be to look over the edge
of my book and see
You sitting in your chair, lost in thought
With the sunset glinting off your hair
A forgotten book or project draped
Carelessly across your lap
Discarded for the moment.

I'd once more trace your profile's features
slowly with my eyes

In a way my fingers still itch to do
Committing every curve to memory
Knowing that there would be
No other way to do so
Now that you're gone.

And even though I know logically the finality of
our parting
I occasionally speak your name out loud
To read you something I've discovered
Some turn of phrase, or a joke
That I know you would share
With me, were our positions reversed.

But our positions, like the sunset,
are irrevocably set
Scheduled by life, unchangeable
And while I would trade places
If only to ease our individual pain
I know that to do so would only
Transfer the loss from me to you.

That loss, forever renewing; constantly
re-opening the wound
Our separation not by choice or chance
But by the fickle finger of fate
Your distance measured
Not in time, or space
But by six feet of earth.

Foggy

There is something beautiful
In the unseen
The misty tendrils that brush our feet
As we scuff through fallen promises of color
Muted by the foggy morning
We've walked this path before
And never seen the floor of leaves
As clearly as we strain now to see it.
Much as we pass through life not really looking
At those around us, those walking next to us
Until tragedy strikes
And they are gone like fog
I turn to you and smile, truly seeing you
And seeing you looking at me smiling as well
The fog is lifted just a little.

Ripple Effect

I told the cashier I liked her earrings
They were funky, fluffy things
They made me smile
She smiled back
The end

Well, at least the end of my part of the day.
The teller smiled at every customer that day
She complimented a grumpy customer
On his tattooed arms
Said they made him look approachable.

He smiled as he left, and held the door
For a tired mom and her cranky toddler
Mid-screaming fit due to missed nap
He told the young mother
You're doing fine- she's two.

The mother left the bank in better spirits
Her daughter gripping a sticky sucker like a trophy
Falling asleep to the motion of the cart
Allowing her mom to see again
The little girl she loved

Just as the burly man had rediscovered
The wonders he'd had engraved on his arms
Reminders of friends and events
Permanently etched in his skin

So familiar he'd stopped seeing them

And the teller who wore the crazy earrings
That her daughter had bought her
For Christmas- a surprise gift
With the money she'd saved all year long
Showing love from her tiny heart

And I, knowing none of this, continued that day
Complimenting people for little things
That didn't really matter to me
Or make my day any better or worse
By hopefully, improving theirs.

Hope

I'd like to talk about endings-
Not the bad, never-read-that-book-again
Ruined-the-movie-hate-the-show
Knee jerk reactionary ending
But the kind where you take a breath
Maybe you smile
And you know, that no matter what
It is over
Finished
Complete
And nothing will ever change that moment

Those endings where you realize
The Prince didn't save the Princess as much as he
Saw her as a way to win a kingdom
And she was ok with that
Preferring to wait until love entered the picture
Whenever that might come

Or the ending where you are shown once again
That no matter the energy
You put into the relationship, the time
The struggle
Sometimes the fairy tale
Simply ends with the words
"And they lived"
No happily ever after
No castle in the clouds like

Some fever dream at a ren faire
Just an end, quiet and basic and right

The thing about an ending
Is that it validates everything that came before
No matter how bad it may have been
How hurtful or hateful or hard
An ending is a reward of a sort- a gift
Like life giving you kudos
For just surviving

Even Pandora still had hope at the end.